# about Bees

ex libris

Candlestick Press

Published by:
Candlestick Press,
Diversity House, 72 Nottingham Road, Arnold, Nottingham NG5 6LF
www.candlestickpress.co.uk

Design and typesetting by Craig Twigg

Printed by Ratcliff & Roper Print Group, Nottinghamshire, UK

Selection © Di Slaney, 2019

Introduction © Brigit Strawbridge Howard, 2019
http://beestrawbridge.blogspot.com/

Cover illustration © Abby Cook, 2019
www.abbycook.co.uk

Candlestick Press monogram © Barbara Shaw, 2008

© Candlestick Press, 2019

Donation to Bumblebee Conservation Trust
www.bumblebeeconservation.org

ISBN 978 1 907598 86 9

**Acknowledgements:**

The poems in this pamphlet are reprinted from the following books, all by
permission of the publishers listed unless stated otherwise. Every effort has been
made to trace the copyright holders of the poems published in this book. The
editor and publisher apologise if any material has been included without
permission or without the appropriate acknowledgement, and would be glad to be
told of anyone who has not been consulted.

Thanks are due to all the copyright holders cited below for their kind permission:

Ciaran Berry, *The Sphere of Birds* (Gallery Press, 2008). By kind permission of
the author and The Gallery Press, Loughcrew, Oldcastle, County Meath, Ireland.
David Briggs, *The Method Men* (Salt, 2010). First appeared in The Poetry Review
Ed. Fiona Sampson Vol 100: 1 Spring 2010, by kind permission of the author.
Miriam Darlington, *Windfall* (Overstep Books, 2008) by kind permission of
Overstep Books Ltd. Heid E. Erdrich, *The Mother's Tongue* (Salt, 2005).
Eamon Grennan, *The Quick of It* (Gallery Press; Graywolf, 2004). By kind
permission of the author and The Gallery Press, Loughcrew, Oldcastle, County
Meath, Ireland. Selima Hill, *Gloria: Selected Poems* (Bloodaxe Books, 2008)
www.bloodaxebooks.com. Carola Luther, *Arguing with Malarchy* (Carcanet
Press, 2011). Paula Meehan, *Geomantic* (Daedalus Press, 2016). Pascale Petit,
*The Treekeeper's Tale* (Seren, 2008). Jean Toomer, *Collected Poems* (University
of North Carolina Press, 1988) by kind permission of Yale University's Beinecke
Collection of Rare Books and Manuscripts.

All permissions cleared courtesy of Swift Permissions
(swiftpermissions@gmail.com).

Where poets are no longer living, their dates are given.

# Contents                                   Page

## Introduction

There's something about honeybees. Something that has, for thousands of years, drawn mankind to want to understand them, care for them, aspire to be more like them, and write poems about them. For some it is the bees' work ethic. For others, the fact that they are master alchemists – guardians of secret recipes and processes that enable them to turn nectar into honey, and pollen into bee-bread, often known as ambrosia, or food of the Gods. For me, it is their 'oneness' – that every task an individual performs is for the greater good of the hive.

As I write, the swarm season is underway, and today I have been watching increasing numbers of scout bees checking out our empty log hive. But other bees enjoy our garden, too. There are buff-tailed bumblebees nesting in the rockery, solitary mining bees burrowing in the lawn, and red mason bees galore emerging from the bee nesting boxes on our walls. The energy of the male mason bees is almost palpable as they dance excitedly around the bamboo tubes, anticipating the emergence of the females. Our whole garden is alive with the buzzing and humming of bees, and there is nowhere else in the world I would rather be. It feels like the clock has stopped and time is standing still. Carola Luther sums this up beautifully in her poem 'I watch the bees slow down the summer'.

I also love David Briggs' memories of a school master keeping bees, and the way Miriam Darlington describes, with complete acceptance, the bittersweet pain of being stung by her bees. "I wear their fury like gloves" she writes. I know this feeling well.

I hope you enjoy this beautiful collection of poems about bees as much as I have.


*Brigit Strawbridge Howard*

# I watch the bees slow down the summer

I watch the bees slow down the summer.  Honeysuckle sink
beneath their substance.  Sunlit busbies stuffed with sleep
and ochre powder making journeys, wavery, vague,
full of just-remembered purpose, so I come to think
of aged gardeners, with their pots and hats and secret
pockets full of dust, casting stuff on yellow air so seconds
stretch (a whole long summer each, if we could only enter them)
a gift of sorts, for us, a hunch, as if they've guessed, the bees,
and understood the rock at the garden's end, the crouching
sky, the path on its narrow belly, dropping to the sea.


*Carola Luther*

## Elegy for the Bee-god

Stingless bees
were bred in tree hollows
for beeswax and honey.
Every year, in the month
called Tzec, the bee-keepers
played their raspadores
and danced across the fields
with bells and ribbons
round their feet, to honour
the fat bee-god, who buzzed
in the heated air
to their music.
He lived in a gold house
in the hotlands, and drank
cocoa sweetened with honey.

All's quiet now, it's June,
and he's not here, the late,
the long-forgotten bee-god,
who sped on zigzag wings
across the sky to the faithful.
Cross-eyed, bejewelled
and tattooed, drumming
his fluffy yellow feet
on the tree hollows,
he gave the bees new hope,
and cocoa sweetened with honey.

If ever I find him – thin,
justly offended, dead
in the dry chaparral –
I will put jade beads
and honey on his tongue,
and wrap him in a shroud
of wings, and loop his neck
with pearls from Guatemala;
I will light him candles
of beeswax, bringing sleep,

and he will rest in the shade
of the First Tree,
and wait for me there –
humming a tune, and drinking
cocoa sweetened with honey.


*Selima Hill*

## Beekeeper

I know each one by heart
feel each hive beat with the need for air
crumple between sheets of cloud
like the rumble of an approaching storm.
When I slide each comb into the light
warm gold crystallises in each struggling socket –
I pour with bees
birthing from their fuzz-world
they cloy like bear fur
a bee blanket wraps me
in a sweet brown buzz
afterwards, bare knuckles pulsing
I wear their fury like gloves.


*Miriam Darlington*

## Stung

She couldn't help but sting my finger,
clinging a moment before I flung her
to the ground.  Her gold is true, not the trick
evening light plays on my roses.
She curls into herself, stinger twitching
gilt wings folded.  Her whole life just a few weeks,
and my pain subsided in a moment.
In the cold, she hardly had her wits to buzz.
No warning from either of us:
she sleeping in the richness of those petals,
then the hand, my hand, cupping the bloom
in devastating force, crushing the petals for the scent.
And she mortally threatened, wholly unaware
that I do this daily, alone with the gold last light,
in what seems to me an act of love.


*Heid E. Erdrich*

# The Bee Mother

I want to go back now, through the buzzing darkness.
I want to go into that humming hive awake,
wearing the net curtain you called my veil.

I want to walk down childhood's garden
as that girl who married her mother,
through the marguerite bed

to that nest, where my bee-queen lies
deep in her brood chamber.
I want to see the honeycomb of your mind.

I want to look into your compound eyes
where I'm reflected as an angry swarm.
I want to be that daughter whose mother has stung her

because she's a rival,
who's still pumping venom into her.
I want to be that childless worker

who dared to sting back, shreds
of my torn abdomen hanging off you
as I leave my stinger behind.

I have cleaned the window of my self until I gleam.
I want you to see how radiant I am
on this, my wedding day.

With all the love I now know,
I want to brush the halo of your hair
and mend the delicate rays of your wings.

I'll place royal jelly in your coffin
for your last flight
and close the moonlit petals of your face.


*Pascale Petit*

## A Beard of Bees

In a scorched July field near Stinson beach
    I watched a man in a white polyester suit
        remove the queen from her wax and amber cell
deep in the hive.  He handled her casually,

    as though she were a chess piece – the carved
        ivory symbol of herself – and not the gnarl
of pheromones that controlled her golden horde
    in their flights among the asters and lupins.

    Gently, stroking her soft back with his thumb,
he placed her in the cage beneath his chin,
    tucking her in before he closed the little hatch
        and stepped backwards, twelve or thirteen paces,

his boots hoof-tapping off the dry, cracked earth
    until he stopped and the whole afternoon
        went still.  Silenced, those of us gathered saw
the five o'clock sun make long his shadow

    over the parched oat grass, the wire fence
        that held, at every barb, knots of goat hair,
the odd magpie or mockingbird feather.
    We waited, observers among the bees,

    our being there reduced to ears and eyes
when the swarm came, at first as a faint drone,
    the turning over of a small engine, then as
        a loose thread spooling from the hive,

the bees unravelling, forming a line
    that covered so quickly the short distance
        between the honeycombs and their trapped queen.
They dipped and landed on the keeper's cheeks,

settled into the beard he wore, mouth almost shut,
      nostrils blocked with cotton wool.  And it struck me
that all of this must be to do with death:
    the way the bees had scrieved across the air,

      their see-through wings thrashing in unison;
the keeper's need to feel against his flesh
    that knot of tangled muscle and barbed sting;
      our need to watch, awestruck, like the rough crowd

at a hanging, as the moment cracked open,
    the field and the minutes suddenly rent,
      unfixed.  We know the queen emasculates
the drone during mating, ripping the phallus

    from his abdomen so that he bleeds to death
      within the hour, but what about the beard of bees,
that thick black mass like a burned out heart,
    alive with malice and ardour, some feral need?


*Ciaran Berry*

# In the Senior Common Room

*A swarm without a hive has no master.*
                    – Law of the Roman Republic

The Divinity master kept bees: his apiary set
beyond the Second Eleven's outfield,
at the gorse-hedged limit of the grounds.
Long, summer afternoons they watched him
going among hives through wedged shadows,
and those who couldn't hold a bat straight

opted 'off Games' to go to the honeybee
and learn how diligent she is.
The breaking of the comb-honey's wax capping
was what they came to cherish –
an Arcadian crème brûlée
they smeared on hot crumpets, spooned into tea

those autumn nights in the oak-panelled study.
He told them bees were blessed when leaving Eden,
became handmaids of the Most High;
how Bretons believed them the tears of Christ crucified;
how they sing 'Hosanna in Excelsis'
on the stroke of midnight each Christmas Eve,

for which he would bless them with slabs of fondant.
They wore the angry blotches on their knuckles
proudly; and, when a swarm of errant drones,
drunk on gorse flowers, flew a careless scrawl
through the lunch hall window,
to rummage among the treacle puddings,

and prompt HM – worn beyond patience
by years of bee-related complaint –
to pronounce, 'Since you cannot control them,
these pests are no more welcome here
than disease,' they replied, 'But
how do you know they're *our* bees?'


*David Briggs*

## Beehive

Within this black hive to-night
There swarm a million bees;
Bees passing in and out the moon,
Bees escaping out the moon,
Bees returning through the moon,
Silver bees intently buzzing,
Silver honey dripping from the swarm of bees
Earth is a waxen cell of the world comb,
And I, a drone,
Lying on my back,
Lipping honey,
Getting drunk with that silver honey,
Wish that I might fly out past the moon
And curl forever in some far-off farmyard flower.


*Jean Toomer (1894 – 1967)*

## Back they sputter

Back they sputter like the fires of love, the bees to their broken home
which they're putting together again for dear life, knowing nothing
of the heart beating under their floorboards, besieged here, seeking
a life of its own.  All day their brisk shadows zigzag and flicker

along a whitewashed gable, trafficking in and out of a hair-crack
under wooden eaves, where they make a life for themselves that knows
no let-up through hours of exploration and return, their thighs golden
with pollen, their multitudinous eyes stapled to a single purpose:

to make winter safe for their likes, stack-packing the queen's chambers
with sweetness.  Later, listen: one warm humming note, their night music.


*Eamon Grennan*

## The January Bee

Who comes to the winter-flowering shrub,
grief in his empty pouches, who sups
alone in the stilled garden this dusk:

I would have missed him only I stopped
mid-argument to watch the moonrise
over the wet roofs of the suburb

and caught him at work deep in the musk,
shaking the bells of the scarce blossoms,
tolling our angers, ringing in peace.


*Paula Meehan*